Donna Kakonge

## **Where I Was**

Donna Kakonge grew up in Toronto and trained as a journalist at Carleton University in Ottawa, Canada from 1990 to 1994. Her first attempt at fiction was a novel she wrote at the age of 17 after reading Danielle Steele and Stephen King, as well as Sweet Valley High books. She did not publish this book, later titled *My Roxanne*, until 2007. She has written many freelance articles and reviews for newspapers, magazines and online sources. Her first published short story came out of a creative writing workshop at Carleton University with Tom Henighan and was featured in *Headlight Anthology* – a Concordia University student-published journal. Kakonge did her MA in media studies at Concordia from 1997 to 1999. She has taught at Carleton and Concordia Universities as a teaching assistant. She has also taught a full course at Concordia University and overseas at Makerere

University in Kampala, Uganda. From 2006 to the present, Kakonge teaches at Centennial College, Seneca College, the University of Guelph-Humber and Humber College, all in Toronto. She has worked as a journalist on and off with the Canadian Broadcasting Corporation from 1992 to 2007. She received a student award from Carleton University as the graduating student with the most promise of becoming an exceptional journalist in honour of the late journalist Marjorie Nichols. She has also received a Gemini nomination for a pilot episode of a television show that aired on the Discovery Channel, plus numerous scholarships to attend the Innoversity Diversity Summit in Toronto. She has also received a Quebecor Documentary Fellowship. Kakonge is also the author of *What Happened to the Afro?*, *How to Write Creative Non-fiction*, *Spiderwoman*, *Morning English Lessons*, *In My Pocket*, editor of *Being Healthy: Selected Works from the Internet*, *Do Not Know*, *My Story of Transportation*, *Draft: eSpirituality*

*Chats*, a CD of radio documentaries called "Nine," *Journalism Stories Collection*, *Digital Journals and Numerology* and two audio stories from *Spiderwoman*, "Matoke" and "Church Sunday." The latter appeared in *Headlight Anthology*. Donna Kakonge lives in Toronto, Canada.

www.donnakakonge.com

# BOOKS AND CDS BY DONNA KAKONGE

What Happened to the Afro?

How to Write Creative Non-fiction

Spiderwoman

My Roxanne

Being Healthy: Selected Works from the

Internet (edited)

Do Not Know

My Story of Transportation

Draft: eSpirituality Chats

"Nine" (CD)

Journalism Stories Collection

Where I Was

Donna Kakonge

Lulu.com

FIRST EDITION LULU INTERNATIONAL

EDITION, December 2008


Copyright 2008 by Donna Kay Kakonge,

M.A.


All rights researched under International

and Pan-American Copyright Conventions.

Published in the United States by

Lulu.com.


National Archives of Canada Cataloguing

in Publication Data

Kakonge, Donna

Where I Was

ISBN: 978-0-9810797-3-8


Book Design by Dreamstime.com


Manufactured in the United States.

To Oshun

"Everybody's gotta story that could break your heart."

~ Amanda Marshall

# WHERE I WAS

Prologue

He was first made visible to me as I stood behind him in the self-serve checkout at the grocery store. He was wearing a red St. Louis Cardinals baseball cap. I am not too picky when it comes to men – they just have to stand out. They have to be attractive to me and good-looking in general. And I have always been a sucker for a man with full lips, chewing gum.

I stood a little too close to him in the line. He kept glancing over at me under the brim of his cap, his face frozen and expressionless. He was hard to read. I looked only at his square jaw, determined not to make eye contact.

I could see how much his bill came to – exactly $40.00. He bought a bag of pretzels, black currant juice, a bag of dried apricots, hummus, cans of black beans and chickpeas, rice and a bag of chewing gum. All I had was a pack of chewing gum. I had been living on chewing gum for the past day.

"Can I eat with you?" I asked him, partly out of attraction, partly because I was hungry.

He looked at me and smiled.

"Are you serious?"

Then our eyes met, mine black and his brown. I nodded.

He shrugged his shoulders and shook his head and walked away, mumbling something like "I don't even know you."

I bought my pack of gum. Shrugging off my own feelings of embarrassment, I left the grocery store to return to my apartment down the street. As I left the store, I saw him heading north at the corner of Lansdowne and Dundas, where the No Frills grocery store is. He was heading to the good part of town. I was heading south towards Queen, where one of the worst buildings in the city is where I called home.

It didn't take me long to get home. The grocery store was a short walk to my building where people would piss in the elevator and write nasty things on the walls. There were security cameras, but they didn't tend to deter people from committing crimes on the premises. There were also security guards, though most of the tenants knew they were in on the illicit activity. What kind of building sold contraband cigarettes in their own convenience store? I didn't even want to know what else they might sell there.

I slammed my door shut and quickly slid the dead bolt, as I had grown accustomed to over the one month I had been living there. I went to my computer that my Dad (who lived in a good part of town) helped me buy. I even had Internet access. It's funny how poverty makes you appreciate things you would have taken for granted before.

I went to Craigslist and considered putting a "missed connection" posting up about the guy I saw at No Frills. I had just recently ended a relationship with someone who helped to put me in this state of financial despair. This new guy was cute and plus, I would love it if he would cook for me.

I decided to post something up there. With the title "Beautiful Black Man at No Frills – w4m", I told him I wanted him to cook for me. After I posted it, I felt stupid and realized I was just crying out for attention. No different than answering the ad in the *Toronto Star* about the commercial, making $3,000 for it, blowing it all, and then taking out a loan to buy a green Jaguar. No different than loaning more money to put a down payment on a condo in Rosedale, pay for acting lessons and basically pretend that I was a black

Paris Hilton living a simple life that really was not that simple. Well, my life was simply dirt poor now. What I needed to do was find a job and get my money situation back on track rather than chase after young men who did not want me. So…this is how I did it.

This is the story of before the day I met the hot man chewing gum. This is the genesis of how I turned from economic mess to economic sense through the power of pen, paper and hands clicking away at a keyboard so I could see through

glasses the screen before me.

I am anointing my new prize, my new stable into writing. I will never grieve the loss of something old, because it means something new is happening. Something different and dramatic is approaching on the horizon.

I would love to get the chance to see Micheline – she has a lot of talent. I would love to get the right to be a billionaire with a few trillion dollars extra so I can go off on lavish vacations and the sort.

I am getting a lot of good advice from those books. A lot of good summaries and quotations of the kind of thing I'll be doing with my life. It will all fall into place – and I'm not lazy. I'm not worried about a thing. Michel knows I'm not the homemaker type. There is just nothing I regret – and I don't even have to turn back time.

Sweet justice, to see me coming in there – high and bothered. I don't know what possessed me, but it was certainly something that I needed to know before I proceeded to the next level. I love myself, I love my choices in life – it's all come down to milk bought at a decent price, available every morning.

You'd get good recommendations and a salary raise if you stayed, but we know you'd rather be somewhere else.

I feel like I'm becoming more of an adult. I was happy when I was younger in my own in the world. I created. I liked school, sometimes, as long as they made it fun. Now I don't have to deal with peer pressure. I'm going to pickup that Girl magazine. I can effectively ward it off. You're going to write a book, completed, published, marketable in a matter of a few days or weeks even. Live a life of adventure. "Eyewitness News" has gotten you long enough.

Write the right way, from your heart. You will take a spirit soul with you every time you say a prayer. It's interesting how much we take into our system when tired. I am thankful to all the women and gay men who have struggled in the writing fields making sure all us brown folk will be able to write.

Who gets published and who doesn't get published is a question of validation. It is a question of who has voice, and who doesn't. Who counts, and who doesn't. At certain times I keep pinching myself that I'm not still sleeping. Will I be a proponent of welfare? The answer is trying to make a living from your guts and glory – from the thing that really makes you shake and sizzle.

This profile reminds me of nothing in fact. I think I'm trying to make too many breaks and pauses.

I must find the peace and serenity to do whatever I want, basing the consequences on a good outcome. Power to me!

I'm thinking of depression. How I will experience it in a new way. It seems to be something that could happen, as my doctor says. Michel told me not to worry. If others could do it, so could I. This need not be a missionary when it comes to doing everything or anything anyone tells me. You will do just fine. Things are easier then they seem. You just need a good day of cleaning, and that will be all right for you.

All I need is a computer table and a writing table. A nice place at a good price. I need these things because if I don't have them then nothing will ever get done. I have to remember I'm a businesswoman, and that this is where my heart lies in many ways.

We who are young adore those who are old – in a land named Nevik. It will be nothing but a Christmas story he can give to the parents of kids who frequent the store.

I love Montreal because my name puts me at an advantage. Many people spell it different ways to hear it.

Think Christmas in June.

Donna, the worst thing you can do right now is invite any tarot card or voodoo into your life. It could be the death of your whole life, your spirit gone for all time. Never use those things again. Disruption

is not in your nature. It's in other people –
but not in yours.

I do think there is a fear of writers. It's
the idea that everything you've ever had
will be revealed. They are watching and
observing.

Why would I want to live around CBC
women. They always make me nervous. I
hope Enid likes the place right away. I
have made a commitment – I'm not just
trying this on for size to see how it fits.

I've been doing this for 20 years. No shortcuts. Interesting routes, yes. I will revel in the road. When I'm ready to bust a move, I will bust a move.

A few things I must remember on this journey – don't let the big ones corrupt you. Never lose your faith. If it feels right, do it, and if it feels wrong, don't.

The fundamental difference between what I do, and what I say are the remarks in between.

I miss Michel. He is my buddy. I'm scared, but I love him. I hope my mother really likes him, and she understands his English.

No regrets. You have worked hard to get to this point. Go on girl, make a few calls.

For Michel:

I miss you baby. I miss you baby. I do enjoy your smile when you're with me. If you could only stop sharing your good news with me, and the plans you're making. But I'll ask you one more time, my dear, don't go.

My conversation last night with Tife was satisfying to say the least. I am conquering my fears, learning not to always be in control. I'm getting better at taking advice from others without cutting out my own desires.

I'm going to apply to McGill again in November. I would feel comfortable there – and I don't care what marks I get. I'll get funding from the Federal Union of Government Assistant Employees if I have to.

She liked Gap clothing, Barbie dolls from the States, and everything else fine and nice. You were never looking for a man who would merely sing your praises or a prejudiced man who would hump your mama. All you needed was a man to say "I love you" at night.

Donna, you are very pretty. Even on your off days, you still command a presence.

If I had a dollar for every time someone has tried to get to know me better because of my sickness, or because of my charm and beauty, well, I could buy most of that stale clothing at The Gap.

You are doing good, girl, really representing on the home scene, too.

I sometimes have this dream that I'll become like Oprah Winfrey – a queen of radio and pop culture, and Michel will be my king.

You have worked well my darling. Putting food on the table of my former roommate Carl sure has been a good thing.

Why are they so angry? Because I don't sit at home eating bon-bons and singing spirituals all day? Save it, it's the rest of the story that gets interesting.

It was a good day. I got a lot of things done. I'm still really scared and missing Michel since he's gone to work again. The most successful thing I think I did today was to send off my text to *Panache*.

I really want to get into the writing program at Humber College. I think it would be great for me.

I've gone through a lot and I've survived. That Greek man was scary, but I made it through. And that black guy was even scarier, but I made it through.

I will always have my journal and God knows I'm thankful for that. The Tweety Bird one from my mother was heaven-sent. And that's why I have to work. I have to work 'till I drop. Just like the

worker bees. I haven't become the Queen

Bee. Yet.

June 19, 2000


I've had a wonderful day. I got everything done. Went to the Unemployment Insurance office, picked up the keys for my beautiful apartment, saw my doctor, which was great. I even paid for my fridge and stove. The best parts were watching Oprah and seeing this large woman overcome her drug addiction and get a fellowship to study writing. She is now going to South Africa to pursue her PhD in

African literature. And she has a child. The story was so inspiring and gave me faith in my future. I would love to study literature too, maybe African-American literature.

Life is a funny thing. Just when you think you don't know where you're going, something comes along to put you on the path you know you want to be on.

I'm going to spend a lot of time on this re-write for *Panache*, making sure it's what they want. And what I want.

Michel's mother just phoned – she's so dear to me. A very sweet woman.

I had a good time with Tiferanji as well. We went to a café down the street from Michel's place and had interesting conversations about many things.

I had a good day dear Lord, thank you.

The sun was shining and I thank you

again for everyone in my life and all that

is to come. For now, I'm happy.

July 10, 2000


Now I am finally moved into my new

apartment.

July 1, 2000

I have so much to be thankful for, praise Jesus. This was the most successful move ever. And yet, I'm so anxious and full of trepidation. Some neighbours I've met seem nice. The one across the hall is from France.

When is Michel coming back? I miss him terribly. It feels so good relaxing on clean sheets. I'm learning to live without stimulants, but I'm beginning to feel like my parents are a lot better than me. My father gave me encouragement, but it's hard. I can hang in there.

I'm going through an interesting phase now. Learning to forgive. Loving Michel and telling myself everything will be alright.

I'll write more later.

Wow, was I angry at Sophie. I will never help anyone again. But it's impossible to do so. It's not feasible. People just take advantage of you. I am still fuming.

OK, I got that out of my system. Now I have to sit here waiting for Caroline. At least I should be getting my way in that affair. She is trying to hold me up on something. I'm mad about that too. I can't stand incompetence. Just utter incompetence. I should be in Jean Talon market getting food. I'm going to have some breakfast now.

Happiness. That is what I'm feeling right now. A total calm and happiness as Mozart plays. I love Mozart. I love my life, Michel, and I love Tiferanji, too. I am so proud of myself that I finished my book and that I have a second one on the way.

I have so many plans and a job now. I'm so happy. And health is a wonderful thing. And I got my cheque from Mairuth and from the Youth Employment services. Things are going well and I cannot complain. My life is full. Michel, that beautiful man, is coming this weekend. Tomorrow in fact. Love is a beautiful thing. I talked to this guy in a store about books today. It was great. Made me feel so enthused. I think I'm going to like doing ESL classes. I have training on Saturday and that is great. I really need this job, just to get out of the house.

Thank you God for all the blessings. I thank you God in every way I can.

I did it again, I finished another book and frankly I think it's excellent. It's bestseller type of material. I'm glad I've finished it now, just before teaching. The writing was also cathartic. I think I sympathize with Roxanne – she is a powerful woman who takes a lot of abuse. The story is complicated, but it is basically about power. It's really quite a sexy book with a lot of intrigue and a story that just keeps pushing ahead. I am proud of myself that I have completed these two books. It shows a lot of productivity on my part. I hope I get the Canada Council and Ontario Arts Council grants. It will depend on a lot of things, and I know what I'm up against.

The next book is going to be even better. And I love my warm apartment now. What will help me sleep? Perhaps getting into Myra's life a bit. There are so many books to read.

My thoughts are floating on the prospects for the future. I'm not going to listen to everything Anthony says, but much of it made sense. I feel empowered, like I have a job to do, and I'm going to do it well. Thank God for Anne Diamond. I think she's going to like my "Lizard in the Yard" story. And perhaps I will have it published in *Geist*. This meeting with Anthony was wonderful. He's truly helpful and he knows so much about me already. He's a new friend, exactly what I need right now.

And Michel, he's wonderful. I can feel the warmth in his voice from so far away.

I'm focusing, making decisions. And I must realize that the multicultural dream died with Trudeau. It's a myth. The hard reality is that there is racism in this country. My identity as a black woman in this province has to be fortified. I can't pretend to be anything but what I am. And I will make no more compromises. I have faith that everything will work out. I'm willing to work on my writing, because my soul expands with each word.

Well, it looks like things are working out. Just as *Panache* is fading away, I've been led to something else that will really help me. I think Anthony and I will cut a deal where he gives me painting lessons in exchange for work on the magazine.

This is a real chance to do what I want to do. It feels right, and it came from Anne Diamond. Caribbeans get things done when it comes to literature in this country. There's groundwork that needs to be laid. Anthony is working in both systems with a clear idea of where he's heading. And the fuzziness will soon lift from my brain, too.

I felt lonely today. Barely anyone called. The phone was dead. But it was calming at the same time. Tomorrow I will see Anna and get more of the human contact I crave.

No one will ever know how much they hurt me when they disrespect me.

They take time out of their day to tell me I'm a lunatic. And the worst thing is that I fear I am. I fear that I'm not strong enough for this world. Whom do I have to prove my strength to? Whom do I have to be strong for? Well the answer is easy. I have to be strong for myself. I have to be strong for my loved ones – as my father has always been strong for me.

I need to clear my mind of the clutter. I knew I would have problems when Michel left. I knew it, and it could only be so easy for him to attend to every need. He has his own life. But what does life mean? Is it about collecting things, or is it about love? We live too short for our time on this planet to be without love. That's what Anthony's jealous of. That's what Gabriel is jealous of. I'm in love. How many people have tried to steal from me in my life? Steal my joy. Even John warned me.

Never say his name again. Never talk about the past again. Why should I be a martyr? Why should I tell my story? I would be a guinea pig. I need to protect my life. Do I even want to?

He loves me, this I know. I love him. I would marry him today if I could. I want the challenges of real life. Marriage, children, mutual loving, commitment. Michel, I love you and I need you and I want to grow old with you. I am truly miserable without you. It's happening again…I ran away the last time the psychotic episode started.

I love Michel, he is so great. I hope the advice he gave me to call Elvira was sound.


God, I want this job at AMARC, but I will leave it to your will. If you think this is the job I need, that would help me, then I ask you to have my angels guide me through that interview. Do you think I'm going to get it?

OK. I leave it in your hands. Being a Medical Health Reporter for CFCF-12 would be excellent. But I leave it in your hands, I leave it to your will whatever you think is best for me. I hope that's OK. I will beg you for nothing more than a job I'd truly enjoy. Thank you.

It's been awhile since I've written, but it always feels good to get back to the page. I am feeling cold here in Quebec City. A lot of snow and wind. Must mean I don't need to talk as much. Michel bought me a beautiful promise ring. Today I did something different with my hair. Yesterday I read the *Four Agreements*. I'm starting to feel like getting back into reading again. I will really try to live by those four agreements, starting today.

I think about my book a lot. Yes, I want to write, but I don't want to be a journalist. I want to write a book about Dolly's café, with its rich characters. I think it would make a really great book. When it comes to my writing – am I living by the four agreements? Am I being impeccable with my word, am I not taking anything personally? Am I not making any assumptions? The best I can do is hope and to pray I did my best work at the time and it is an honest place of work. I think I'm going to send my book to Arsenal Pulp Press. I could of done more research when I was at Pages to see what they had on manic depression. But, if it didn't come to mind, there must be a reason for it. I feel tired, but I still have the urge to write. My eyes feel like they're welling up with tears,

I have so many fears. But none of them is going to come true. I am going to be with Michel for the rest of my life. I am not going to have a father who is going to commit suicide as the psychic said. And I am going to live in Heaven right here on earth.

Michel gave me the best ring in the world. He's sleeping now and I'm lying here beside him for one of the few last times before he goes to France. I pray all will go well for both of us.

I have read *The Holy Bible*, and I have read extraordinary things. I have also read *The Four Agreements*. Pretty heady stuff.

Maybe I did have a breakdown from reading too much. Maybe I already have the answers but cannot accept the question.

Michel is leaving for eight months. It may seem like a year, or only a few days.

Probably the former. It really feels good to be writing all this down.

I would like to do my PhD. I like research. I like thinking, I like writing, and I guess I just feel uncertain because I'm not sure what I would get out of it in the end. God will help me.

Do I forgive God? Do I forgive God for bringing me what many others perceive as bad luck? Haven't I been surviving? Haven't I learned a lot about myself?

I am extremely intrigued by Ruiz's notion that mental illness is based on fear, and that once we forgive all of those we believe have done us wrong, including God, we can start healing. I am very intrigued by that and I think it would make a fascinating point of study. A PhD in the humanities, concentrating on communication, creative writing and religion.

Is it true that through forgiving God, the mentally ill can be healed? What proof of this is there? And is propagating this kind of idea damaging to the medical treatment of the mentally ill. No, this is religion and psychology…that is all.

I love Michel. I hope that man has a safe journey. Taking the poison out is such a good idea. Taking out the poison. It's like a north-south debate – it even relates to international communication, but I like doing it in the humanities.

Imagine if I find my cure. Imagine if I find the way to heal myself. Could this all be possible? I'm very tired, but I don't want to go to sleep. Am I angry with Daddy once again that he didn't have the money to make one of my big dreams come true. That's yet to be decided any way. I can rest with that and let it go. Can I forgive myself for not going to France right now? It would have been too easy to go. I would have been doing it out of fear. I love Michel and an ocean doesn't change that at all.

If I only had one dream for the two of us, it would be that we would never part. We would always stay together like that ring around my finger, the stones, never to part. I love that man so much. I think especially because there is so much boy in him. I love his beautiful ways. Thank you God for bringing him to me. I will be forever grateful.

I just feel an impeccable need to pour out all of my sin. The holidays were great, I had a wonderful time. I wish they could happen again.

God, please find me a cure to my mental illness and any other health problems I may have. I ask for your guidance, for your assistance. I will do whatever it takes as long as it is a peaceful path that brings me joy, success, and most importantly, a greater love for all things. May Michel rest peacefully tonight and do well in his studies. May my father be peaceful.

Jewelry does matter to me. I love it and it makes me feel good. It's a beautiful thing and I'm a beautiful woman and I deserve it.

My medication is not a crutch. It helps me stay well. I am strong and full of energy with it.

Thank you God for lending me this book. I will keep it as long as long as I can. Thank you again for everything you have given to me. My sheets feel fine.

An inventory of the mitote:

I am a bad person when I don't do something right.
I have become an old woman by not going out and partying more.
Black men are bad.
My sister does not love me.

I speak French well.

I spend too much money.

I hate to be busy.

I'll never find a job in writing that would satisfy me.

Academia is filled with stuffed shirts who just want money.

I can get off my medication and this would make me a better person.

I'm too serious.

I'm too generous.

My hair will not grow.

I need expensive things for my face, skin and hair.

I hope I will be perfect skin some day because I believe my skin is not perfect now.

If I don't take my medication, I will have a breakdown.

The medication is screwing with my body.

Tarot is evil.

My book will never get published.

Masturbating is bad.

I hate it when I don't fall dead asleep.

These are examples from the *Four Agreements* of the kinds of negative thoughts that stick in my brain.

I spend so much time alone, but I must learn to enjoy it. I have faith – nam myo renge must learn to enjoy this time I have to myself because it probably, always won't be this way. Things are quiet, I'm grateful for my warm bed, for my body, my hair, and my health. I have set the alarm. I think I'm going to have to make a conscious effort to keep toxic people like Bob out of my life. He reminds me too much of a place where my father was. I'm going to tell him that. Sometimes being with him is so depressing that I'd rather be alone.

I had this dream that I got married to my cousin Benjamin and I didn't like it.

My Dream Job:

I want flexible hours.

I want to be able to write.

I want to be close to work.

I want to make a good income.

I want to work with people I like.

I want a boss who I respect and get along with.

I do want a job where I can dress well within reason.

I want lots of holiday time.

I want the chance to travel.

I want a great social life outside work.

I want to be able to live with Michel wherever I work.

I want the chance to work in arts and entertainment.

I want the chance to join a band and sing along with my work.

I want an excellent benefit plan.

I want the chance to grow in the company.



I don't want to work too many late nights.

I don't want to work in a gossipy environment.

I don't want a job that is going to conflict with my medical care – especially with Dr. Wiviott.

I don't want an unstable job.

I don't want a job that is not going to advance my writing career.

I don't want a job that is going to consume all my time.

I don't want a job where I can't be with Michel on a full-time basis.

I don't want a job that may lead me to a mental breakdown.

It's amazing how some Americans can't even spell my name, even when they work in a bookstore.

I'm thinking about my book, making sure it gets published. I should take nothing personally. (That's directed towards my father and mother.) I have to get in touch with Debbie and find out about her place. I should talk to Angela and her friend as well, though it would only be a temporary situation until Michel comes back.

Sometimes I just don't know what Michel is thinking. And it unnerves me because I don't know if he's upset with me or not. I'm reading this part out loud to him, and he's saying nothing. He even walked away.

How do you get inside someone's head if they don't seem to want you there?

It's proving tricky to rent the apartment. I hope everything goes well. I'm listening to Erykah Badu right now. It's a bit disturbing, this first song, because I have up loud. But it helps to drown out my negative thoughts. I hope it's not too loud for my neighbours.

I am feeling more and more like I need to move. Get away from this. Am I running? I think not. I just can't afford this anymore, I really can't. This is the last

day of that bogus French course I have
taken.

Forgiveness:

I ask Daddy to forgive me.

I ask Mommy to forgive me.

I ask Lisa to forgive me.

I ask Kevin to forgive me.

I ask Lisa Watson to forgive me.

I ask Chris Dolson to forgive me.

I ask Auntie Lillian to forgive me.

I ask Jason Yip to forgive me.

I ask the CBC to forgive me.

I ask my body to forgive me.

I ask David to forgive me.

I ask Kim to forgive me.

I ask Laura to forgive me.

I ask Ginette to forgive me.

I ask Ousseynou to forgive me.

I ask Tiferanji to forgive me.

I ask Michel to forgive me.


I ask that drunk man to forgive me.

I ask all the doctors to forgive me.

I ask Auntie Betty and my family in Uganda to forgive me.

I ask Sophie Pascale to forgive me.

I ask Enid to forgive me.

I ask anyone I've ever judged automatically to forgive me.

I ask the CLC office to forgive me.

I ask Christophe to forgive me.

I ask Sue to forgive me.

I ask Edgna to forgive me.

I ask Roz to forgive me.

I ask Mairuth to forgive me.

I ask Zinzi to forgive me.

I ask Anna to forgive me.

I ask Sophie Sun to forgive me.

I ask Peggy to forgive me.

I ask all the men I've dated and treated badly to forgive me.


I forgive Connie.

I forgive Daddy.

I forgive myself.

I forgive God.

I forgive the CBC.

I forgive Mommy, Kevin, and Lisa.

I forgive Auntie Lillian and all my Ugandan family.

I forgive Uncle Alban.

I forgive Sophie.

I forgive Tife.

I forgive all my friends who've deserted me.

I forgive the doctors.


I forgive myself for anything in a past life.

I forgive Dr. Wiviott.

I forgive the homeopathic and natural doctors.

I forgive Enid.

I forgive Chris.

I forgive Ngaire and Wilson.

I forgive the professors at all my schools.

I forgive myself.

I forgive God.

I'm in Toronto now and a lot of things have been on my mind. I just hate my mother sometimes, although I know she means well. This weight thing is really starting to bother me. I can feel that I am becoming obsessed with the scale. My eating is bothering me. I wonder whether I am eating the right things. My sleep is bothering me. I do get to sleep, but often it's late and now that I'm working it's so difficult to get up in the morning. I feel bad that I haven't called Laura, she probably would really like to talk right now. Work is good, I must stay content, but there is this girl at work who I just don't like. She rubs me the wrong way, and I think she's full of herself.

I'm sorry I got off part of my medication. Maybe it would have worked the way it did when I went to the hospital to see Dr. Wiviott. I don't want to break down again and I'm afraid that may happen. I miss Michel terribly. He is so much of my support. I even miss Dr. Wiviott, he was a joy to talk to. Dr. Jamal is good, and I think she will be a very good doctor, but it's taking me awhile to get into the flow.

There are always all these scenarios moving around in my mind before I go to sleep. I keep thinking of things, mulling things over – my mind's not at rest. I know this isn't a very good sign. The smoking, the coffee, its all bad for me, but I'm reluctant to stop. At least the coffee is under control, and the smoking has improved, but there are still so many improvements that could be made.

Today I feel a lot better, more confident more sure of myself, more in control, my thoughts are clearer.

I asked to work on the syndication desk today because it looked like the work on the hourlies might run out for me for awhile. And I wanted to take things into my hands, so I did.

I feel peaceful. It's 12:30 in the morning and I'm tired but peaceful. I found out that Marilyn lives at Bathurst and Bloor – I like her. Didn't talk to that other girl today, thank God. Met someone who knows the P-word – the bitch, the P-word I mean. Oh well, I guess she's used to using black people.

I had a wonderful walk today –. I walked from Broadview and Danforth home, it took about an hour and a half. I did some good work today, plus, I covered my ass by getting that syndication training. I don't know how many days it will be, but I hope it will be a lot.

I feel like I could sleep forever – but I don't think I will.

I've got to keep remembering to not to be concerned about the insignificant stuff. People in Montreal are really different when it comes to weight. But I feel good about what I'm doing. I think it's the best thing and it's really clearing my head.

I'm looking forward to not getting a ride from Daddy anymore. It will give me a little more independence. Then of course when I think of something Catherine said today, I think maybe she heard about that Culture Shock thing.

My battle with the bulge continues. After going up and down all week I am finally at 201 today. So overall, since last week, I have gained 1.5, but overall lost 3.5 pounds.

I have other plans too. This weekend I hope to clean up my room so I can work on my abdominals every day. I'm actually thinking about doing some walking this weekend. It's supposed to be a nice weekend, so I plan to take advantage of it.

It really pissed me off this evening when Daddy came upstairs and turned out my light then closed my door. Fuck him – who is he to come into my room.

I can hear movie music playing in the background – it sounds so wonderful. I wonder what they're watching. The workweek went well, I'm satisfied with the job I did.

I'm not feeling really good right now. I'm not that happy about how I'm doing at work or how I did today. I felt like a novice. And I hate young white women editors. I find that no matter how nice they try to be, they are always overly critical of a black woman's work. But I must not take anything personally. This is a new start in an old place and I have to get used to the learning curve. There was this other girl there Nancy who really blew me off my feet – I should feel happy for her, but I feel jealous instead. It was nice talking to Bill today, he is a really good man. I like him.

You've done well, kiddo. You've come far. Not many people could say the same thing. You also looked great today and it is nice to be reacquainted with old friends.

People were really helpful and it was a good atmosphere. I guess I just have to try a little harder.

And actually what Lisa said was really helpful. It was kind of her to sit me down and explain everything.

Thank you diary, I feel a lot better.

God, maybe it's just me and I started smelling it, but this guy sat down in the chair I normally sit in and after I sat down in it, it really stank. But then, it's been days since I've really put any soap on my skin. Daddy was asking me all these questions about Laura and I felt really uncomfortable answering. I felt like it really put me on the spot. I'm not sure why, I guess I just don't want to be discussing her business. I've had a quiet day, quite quiet. Got to talk to some people, got some walking in. Saw Dr.

Jamal. It was a good day. Now, I'm going to get some good sleep and rest well.

Oh well, things aren't going very well right now. The CBC hasn't been calling me, I put work today in applying for other jobs. I feel my confidence is kind of low. I'm trying to keep my spirits up. Some things are OK, there's always TV, and the book I wanted has come in at the library. Plus, I found a way to be connected to the Internet through AOL for three months. My sleep is still quite fractured. I don't know, I don't feel satisfied and I really wish I were in South Africa with Michel. I feel quite sad, but I'm sure this will pass and I'll feel better.

Lisa just left without saying goodbye and I'm in the house by myself and I feel alone. I feel a pain in my stomach and anxiety. Discomfort. When did I learn this feeling?

My head is starting to hurt and I understand completely why Paris is taking those painkillers. It's hard to feel pain. It's hard to feel lonely. Sometimes I want to die. I think to myself that it would just be easier. And then no, I have to keep turning the page, find out what happens next. How I can solve some things, on my own or with help would be even better. Am I burnt out at 28? I still feel 21. This can't be good.


I went out with Mommy and Lisa, and I feel a lot better now.

I'm having those suicidal thoughts again. Suffering from low self-esteem. I feel really bad that I got blood on Mommy's cushions. Safia's right though, I am lucky I can live my family. I've been having all sorts of daydreams before I go to bed at night.

Last night, I was think that Sting came to my door so we could work on a documentary about manic depression. Perhaps the real question is: Am I just lazy? It is such an ugly four-letter word. I feel like I'm living like an older person.

OK, it starts with one breath. Knowing life is in your body is exactly how I can get through the day. There are things I want to do, accomplish and have.

I've had this journal for a while and now it's coming to an end. I'm a little scared right now because I can't find my clippings. I just have to have faith that will turn up. My mind is in a bit of a mess.

I would love to fax off some résumés but Lisa has taken her printer into her room. I think, or maybe David has it. Her computer doesn't work very well, so it's difficult for me to send out anything. I guess I could always send it as an email attachment. Wow, I just thought of that. That is a great idea. And, if worse comes to worse, I'm sure I have my articles on disk and I can just explain my situation. That's doing my best, and the best is what I can do. I feel a lot better, a lot more calm. I also applied to The Flight Centre

today. I enjoyed filling out the application.
Thanks journal for helping to clear my
mind.

Well, I applied to the Vision TV job. I think
I would be good at it. I'm still really
nervous about not finding my clippings for
that *Toronto Star* job. I am so grateful
that I have a job that will give me some
money. I'm developing a certain ease with
writing. The experiences we are in are
important, and I can learn a lot from
Olivene. I look forward to seeing Vivian

today. I'm just sitting here hoping for the sun to come up. I think Zinzi is lovely and I hope everything is OK for her and her father.

Here is the end. I'm coming to the turning point. I'm scared. I like working and I find it interesting. I washed my hair today and that felt good. I miss having hair though and a slim body. I'm not sure where these insecurities are really stemming from.

Epilogue

I write this as a listen to a CD called "Manitoba," a collection of Aboriginal artists. It is December 19, 2008 and a lot has changed.

The things that used to bother me before, no longer bother me. I am not worried about my weight – although I am plump. I am happy to be plump.

I have been reading the Bible religiously and I am somewhere in Proverbs. It has been a great source of strength for me. Also, I do believe it has been improving my relationship with God, with those people around me and with myself.

I live next door to my Dad and I am gainfully employed. Many of those desires I set out to have that have been stated in this book have been achieved. I truly believe that anyone can get anything they want in life, as long as what they want will not hurt other people or them. This book is about where I was before I moved back to Toronto nearly eight years ago. Where am I now?

I love life. I am a much more positive person. I do not feel that a man needs to complete me and I have been flying solo romantically for quite some time. I am better about my money – back to the way I used to be. I care about other people and I am less insular. Teaching has really helped me with that. Giving back and getting paid to do that is one of the greatest gifts God has given to me.

Once I discovered the power of self-publishing, my fears of ever getting published diminished. Lulu.com has been a true saving grace for me. Although I do not see my books in Chapters or Indigo, I do see them online…the new frontier. I even have a book on Amazon.com that is published by Lulu.com.

Anything that has been thrown into my path as a problem – I have tried to make it a triumph. Growing up really helps too. Keeping positive people around me really helps as well.

This book is dedicated to my niece Oshun who will be celebrating her second birthday in March 2009. May you understand that things may not always be easy, however I am such a firm believer that in life the best way to deal with it is with these thoughts: "Life is 10 per cent what happens to you and 90 per cent how you react to it." I did not say those wise words, however it was probably something revised from the Bible.

**Also By Donna Kay Kakonge:**

*What Happened to the Afro?*

This graduate research paper is a case study that sheds light on the politics of black hair.


*How to Write Creative Non-fiction*

Writing is one of the hardest jobs in the world, and this book will give you the help you need to crack the market. Everything you wanted to know about the writing business and how to write, with exercises included.

***Spiderwoman***

This book of short stories crafted over many years and originally developed in a writing workshop at Carleton University includes the experiences of a young black woman in Canada, experiencing everything from travel to family tragedy and love.

***My Roxanne***

Written at the age of 17 and revised later in life, this novel is the story of Roxanne

and Lance – an interracial couple who go
through their ups and downs.

### *Being Healthy: Selected Works from the Internet*

This book is a compilation of works from the Internet related to health that have been edited by Donna Kakonge.

### *Do Not Know*

This book is a collection of literary explorations of madness. A young black woman experiences the challenges and adventures of mental illness.

## My Story of Transportation

This book is a memoir of Donna Kakonge's transportation experiences. Everything from roller skates to Jaguars, this is a story of how she has managed to get around.

## Draft: Spirituality Chats

On a desperate search for a PhD, Donna Kakonge actually produces doctorate-level work by discovering there is more knowledge in one's common sense than meets the third eye of psychics.

### *Journalism Stories Collection*

From newspapers and magazines such as NuBeing International, Panache, Pride, Share and the Toronto Star – Donna Kakonge creates a collection of her journalistic stories that span five years of her writing career.

### *The Education Generation*

Perfect for professors, students and anyone in the college or university system in North America, this book has articles and columns that explore the notion of the education generation.

### *Digital Journals and Numerology*

This book is meant to emphasize how powerful keeping a journal can be with the aid of numerology. I started writing one at the age of seven and keeping a journal has been a constant for me – more than some friends, some jobs and some family members. I used to get a thrill selecting my journals to write in. Now I have decided to try something new by using the computer that I already spend so much time on and money on to show how powerful keeping any journal...even a digital journal can be. Using the principles of numerology can also help in chronicling your life.

**Other Work:**

**"Nine"**

This is a selection of some of Donna Kakonge's radio documentaries done with the Canadian Broadcasting Corporation, as well as Radio Canada International.

**"Matoke"**

This audio book brings the story of Matoke from the book Spiderwoman to your ears.

**"Church Sunday"**

From the book Spiderwoman comes an audio story of the story "Church Sunday," first published in Concordia University's *Headlight Anthology* and reviewed by the *Montreal Gazette*.

**In My Pocket**

This book was written to help you during the perilous times we live in.

**Morning English Lessons

This is a book that is ideal for helping you

hone your English skills.

Milton Keynes UK
Ingram Content Group UK Ltd.
UKHW040706050124
435493UK00001B/273